SPRING BULBS

SPRING BULBS

AN ILLUSTRATED GUIDE TO VARIETIES, CULTIVATION AND CARE, WITH
STEP-BY-STEP INSTRUCTIONS AND OVER 120 INSPIRATIONAL PHOTOGRAPHS

Peter McHoy

Photography by Peter Anderson

southwater

This edition is published by Southwater
an imprint of Anness Publishing Ltd
108 Great Russell Street, London WC1B 3NA
info@anness.com

www.southwaterbooks.com; www.annesspublishing.com

If you like the images in this book and would like to investigate
using them for publishing, promotions or advertising, please visit
our website www.practicalpictures.com for more information.

A CIP catalogue record for this book is available from the British Library.

Publisher: Joanna Lorenz
Senior Editor: Clare Nicholson
Editor: Margaret Malone
Designer: Bill Mason
Production Controller: Pirong Wang

PUBLISHER'S NOTE
Although the advice and information in this book are believed to be accurate and true at the time
of going to press, neither the authors nor the publisher can accept any legal responsibility or liability
for any errors or omissions that may have been made nor for any inaccuracies nor for any loss,
harm or injury that comes about from following instructions or advice in this book.

■ HALF TITLE PAGE
Hippeastrum 'Solomon'
■ FRONTISPIECE
Narcissus 'Dutch Master'
■ TITLE PAGE
Narcissus poeticus 'Actea'

■ LEFT
Ornithogalum umbellatum
■ OPPOSITE LEFT
Hyacinthus orientalis 'Hollyhock'
■ OPPOSITE RIGHT
Tulipa 'Ballade'

Contents

Introduction

Bulbs are nature's own ready-to-bloom packages, just waiting to burst into leaf and flower when the time is right. Spring-flowering bulbs are especially wonderful because the early ones emerge even before winter is over, the leaves pushing their way through the sometimes frozen ground.

With few exceptions, these bulbs can be planted in the sure knowledge that they will herald the coming season with a brilliant, multi-coloured display, sweeping away any lingering memories of those bleak winter days. They also bridge the gap until the border perennials and summer annuals take over.

The pictures in this book provide a taste of the delights that come with growing spring bulbs, and the practical advice ensures the success of your own super spring display.

■ RIGHT
Tulipa praestans 'Fusilier' has up to six flowers on a stem.

What is a bulb?

Not all the plants we loosely call bulbs are true bulbs – some are corms, tubers or rhizomes. In this book the term bulb is used in its general sense to include other forms of dried, dormant, underground storage organs normally sold by bulb merchants, though the precise terms (corms, tubers etc) have been used where applicable.

True bulbs are easily identified if cut through with a knife: they have scales like immature leaves arising from a base plate (effectively a small stem), from which the roots emerge. The stems and flowers emerge from the top of the bulb. The scales are normally enclosed in an outer dry, peeling or flaking skin (the tunic),

as in the onion or tulip, though this is not obvious in all bulbs.

Sometimes the scales are not wrapped like this but are clearly visible and sometimes fleshy: lilies are familiar examples.

Corms are really the swollen remains of last year's stems. They may be rounded or flattish, and if cut through lack the typical onion-like rings of a bulb. The roots emerge from the base and the new stem from the top; the corm also contains an embryo flower shoot. The original storage organ (corm), dries up each year, but a new one is formed on top of the old one. Tiny cormlets form around the base of a mature corm, and are used for propagation.

Tubers, like corms, are formed of thickened stem tissue, but the embryo flower shoot within is lacking. Instead they have 'eyes' (small buds) on the upper surface which grow into shoots.

There is another kind of tuber, called a root tuber, which is a swollen root (the potato is a good example). In neither case are there any signs of internal organs when the tuber is cut through.

Rhizomes are fleshy stems which usually grow underground, but they may creep along the surface, as do some summer-flowering irises. New growth emerges from the tip, and roots from along the base. Rhizomes vary considerably in size and shape.

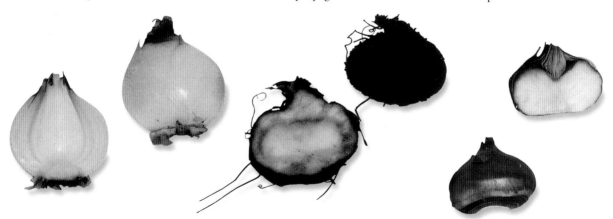

■ A B O V E

Most of the bulbs planted for spring flowering are likely to be true bulbs (like the scilla, shown *above left,* in two halves), tubers (such as the eranthis, *centre*) or corms (such as the crocus, *right*). Their internal structure and external shape give vital clues. True bulbs have onion-like leaves within them, while corms have solid flesh and usually a regular outline like a bulb. Tubers also have solid flesh within, but their outline and shape is often more lumpy and irregular.

Versatility

Like most plants, bulbs repay a little extra care and attention with more flowers and a longer life, but most are also extremely tolerant of neglect if you only require a short-term display. Hyacinths and some daffodils (which include a huge range of forms and colours, not just the traditional yellow trumpet shape), will flower with their roots in nothing more than water, and others can be induced to flower with just a little potting soil around their roots, but they will not flower again the following year unless the bulb is replenished with nutrients.

Because true bulbs of sufficient size already have the embryo flower within them, they will bloom in unpromising shady positions or in poor, impoverished soil. But for a repeat performance that improves year on year they do need suitable conditions and proper care. Any effort, however, is amply repaid by the sight of spring bulbs in bloom.

■ A B O V E
Part of the Keukenhof gardens near Lisse, Holland, the showplace for the Dutch bulb industry and one of the finest places in the world to see spring-flowering bulbs. It is open to the public in spring.

Many spring-flowering bulbs thrive at the edge of deciduous woodland, as they make their growth early and begin to die back before the tree canopy begins to reduce light levels. Most of them require plenty of moisture, however, and they may not thrive in the very dry soil beneath dense tree cover.

The international bulb trade

Holland is the centre of an international trade for spring-flowering bulbs. It has the ideal soil and climate, and the Dutch growers have tremendous expertise in the propagation and production of bulbs.

Around the world there are other centres of excellence for specific bulbs – the USA is famous for its lily production – while a small number of bulbs are grown in other countries, such as the UK.

Cultivated or wild?

Today, most bulbs are propagated and grown in nurseries, and are then exported for sale around the world. Some however, are collected from the wild, especially plants such as *Cyclamen coum.* Cheap labour in the countries where such wild plants are plentiful makes it economic to pay the transport costs, while giving native workers an income. But

■ ABOVE
A spring display like this, with a mix of hyacinths and compact varieties of tulips and narcissi, is as colourful as any summer bedding, but plant closely for maximum impact.

■ RIGHT
Hardy cyclamen is one type of bulb that used to be widely collected from the wild, but nowadays this is discouraged. Reputable bulb merchants only sell cultivated stock.

The Lisse area of Holland is where many of the Dutch bulbs are grown, and in spring the flowers stretch for almost as far as the eye can see. Although some are allowed to flower, the blooms are sometimes removed to divert all the plant's energy into producing bigger bulbs.

collecting from the wild also depletes scarce wild stocks and will eventually endanger the bulbs.

International concern over this wild bulb trade has put pressure on the bulb importers to select only cultivated stock, and many reputable bulb merchants now make a point of labelling relevant bulbs 'from cultivated stock'. If you see this tag, you can confidently buy, knowing that wild plants are not being depleted.

In some areas where collection from the wild used to be practised, the bulb collectors are being retrained to propagate and cultivate the plants so that they still have an income – but one that will not eventually result in the extinction of wild plants.

A wide range of bulbs

The vast majority of bulbs are bred, propagated and distributed by specialist growers, particularly in Holland. They are sometimes sold direct, but usually are distributed world-wide through bulb merchants who distribute in individual countries. Although some popular varieties may be available in many different countries, the number of varieties is so great that not all are universally available, and each year a few are dropped to make way for new ones. If a particular variety mentioned in this book is unavailable, you will almost always be able to buy a similar one.

The varieties mentioned are just examples of the enormous range available. A single supplier may offer over 100 different daffodils and 50 crocuses, for example, and specialist growers might offer a dozen varieties of the common snowdrop (*Galanthus nivalis*), and many more hybrids. Some of the variations are minor, however, and the popular, widely available names are likely to be the best for general garden use.

Naturalizing bulbs

The easiest and most trouble-free way to grow bulbs is in short grass, a technique known as naturalizing. Quite simply, they are planted and left to grow and multiply, often forming large sheets of colour where conditions are particularly suitable.

Tall-growing bulbs are also suitable for a wild garden, while snowdrops and erythroniums prefer woodlands and orchards.

Creating a natural look

Finding a suitable position in which to naturalize your bulbs means you will probably have to compromise.

Naturalized spring bulbs look terrific in the lawn while they are in flower, but nature never intended that they should have their leaves mown off soon after the blooms fade. The foliage helps to feed and sustain the bulbs, and ensures they are in a fit condition to flower the following spring. Cutting off the leaves prematurely will almost certainly prevent flowering the following

season, and will slowly kill the bulbs if repeated for several seasons.

Bulbs are best naturalized in grass that can be left unmown for about 12 weeks after flowering, and are better in a grassy bank than an ornamental lawn. If the lawn is large, though, plant in a few bold drifts where the grass can be left long until summer, while the rest is mown routinely. A colourful carpet of spring bulbs looks superb around a deciduous tree, and leaving the grass long here looks more natural than several patches in the middle of an otherwise beautifully manicured, striped, ornamental lawn.

Wildlife areas in a large lawn are ideal places in which to naturalize bulbs. This particularly applies to a lawn formed from meadow grass, or one sown as a utility lawn where a few rough spots with weeds are acceptable. The merry white faces of daises are charming rather than challenging. If large ovals or irregularly shaped areas with smooth, rounded edges of the lawn are left uncut until mid- or late summer, many native wild flowers will become established – perhaps even wild orchids – and planted spring bulbs such as daffodils and *Fritillaria meleagris* will add to the charm.

■ RIGHT
Banks like this are ideal for naturalizing bulbs such as daffodils. It does not matter if the grass grows long while the bulb foliage dies back naturally.

■ BELOW

Anemone blanda is perfect for naturalizing in front of or among shrubs, or beneath deciduous trees. After a few years it will create a carpet of blue (sometimes white or pink) in early spring.

The long grass and the seedheads that develop will also encourage wildlife such as butterflies and birds.

Grassed orchards beg for bulbs to be planted. Spring bulbs usually thrive if planted in apple or pear orchards because they do most of their growing and flowering before the leaves of the trees unfurl, creating an overly shady habitat.

Borders and banks

Steep banks that are difficult to mow, and roadside banks sometimes found outside rural properties, can be cut less frequently and are sometimes best left entirely natural. If the long grass is cut down once in late summer or early autumn, the wild flowers will have a chance to shed their seeds and multiply, and a tangle of long, dead stems will not mask the new, spring flowers. Daffodils are ideal for planting in this position.

Also try naturalizing low-growing bulbs such as *Anemone blanda* and *Muscari armeniacum* in a shrub border. They will form pleasing rivers of colour in spring when deciduous shrubs are still bare and unispiring, then melting into the background when the shrubs begin to perform in the summer.

Bulbs in beds and borders

Beds used for summer annuals can be just as colourful in spring. Certainly, the flowers of some bulbs are short-lived compared with summer flowers (often no more than a week or two at perfection), but this shortcoming is easily rectified by interplanting them with spring-bedding plants such as winter-flowering pansies, forget-me-nots and polyanthus. They ensure a superb display for more than a month, by which time the beds will probably have to be cleared when the ground is prepared for summer flowers.

Herbaceous and mixed borders also benefit from a generous scattering of bulbs to help provide colour and interest until the late spring, when the early summer plants take over. The emerging shoots relieve the depression of bare soil long before the blooms burst open.

Formal beds

For formal spring bedding, choose bulbs such as daffodils, hyacinths and tulips that can be relied upon for a full-blown display in their first

■ LEFT
Tulips and spiky blue camassias are used lavishly in this mixed border of shrubs and herbaceous plants.

■ RIGHT
The double late
tulip 'Mount
Tacoma' with
Bellis perennis
'Roggli Rose'.

■ FAR RIGHT
Try planting two
kinds of bulbs
together. Here
Scilla siberica has
been planted
between 'Pink
Pearl' hyacinths.

season. Some, like winter aconites
(*Eranthis hyemalis*) and *Anemone
blanda*, may only put on a mediocre
performance the first season, and are
best used where they can form part
of a permanent display.

Interplant bulbs with bushy
bedding plants, such as pansies,
forget-me-nots, double daisies (*Bellis
perennis*), polyanthus or dwarf
wallflowers with late-flowering tulips.
These bedding plants hide the bare
soil, and make tall-stemmed bulbs
like tulips less ungainly and
vulnerable to wind damage.

Such schemes offer scope for
colour co-ordination and

combinations that vary from the
subtle to the gaudy. For example, pale
pink hyacinths, and white or pale
yellow polyanthus make a restful,
receding combination, while deep
blue hyacinths with deep yellow
polyanthus make an arresting sight
that demands attention.

If in doubt about colour
combinations, bear in mind that
white or blue will go with almost
any other colour, and look good.
Pastel shades are forgiving colours.
The ones to be careful with are
brilliant orange and strong magenta
which could look disconcerting
in juxtaposition.

Also beware of planning clever
plant combinations on paper – it is
essential that they flower at the same
time, otherwise the effort is pointless.
Avoid the problem by copying or
modifying succesful, harmonious
combinations that you have seen
in books or in other gardens.

Border planting is easier.
Generally, bold clumps of a single
variety work best, and if the clumps
or drifts are used to fill gaps they will
probably be well spaced out with
little risk of colour clashes. It is often
possible to plant them between
perennials that will hide the dying
foliage as they emerge.

Bulbs in containers

An empty container in winter or spring is a lost opportunity. Once the summer flowers are over they should be replanted with bulbs. Tubs, troughs, window boxes, and even hanging baskets and wall pots, can all be replanted for spring colour.

There are three keys to success with bulbs in containers: choosing appropriate plants for the style and size of container; planting densely; and replanting with fresh bulbs each year, if necessary.

Striking a balance

Most spring-flowering bulbs can be grown successfully in a container. Some are intrinsically more suitable for a one-off seasonal display, while others are better as long-term plants in a large container, left undisturbed for several seasons, perhaps near the base of a tree or shrub.

The container should always be in proportion to the plant. Hyacinths and low-growing tulips like *Kaufmanniana* and *Greigii* hybrids

■ RIGHT
Densely planted narcissi look pleasing in patio pots, but give tall varieties a sheltered position, otherwise they may be damaged by strong winds.

look better in a low, dish-shape container than a tall, narrow one, for example. Tall daffodils and tulips have sufficient height to look good in large pots and tubs.

As a rule of thumb, it is best to use a container not much deeper than the height of the main plant, though this can be interpreted loosely where smaller plants are to fill the gaps and harmonize with the main plant.

All kinds of unusual and interesting containers can be used, perhaps painted or decorated in a colour to match the flowers. But do create drainage holes so that the soil does not become waterlogged.

Close planting

One of the commonest mistakes is planting bulbs too far apart. When planting distances are given with the bulbs, they normally allow space for the bulbs to multiply and spread. Do not increase these distances. When bulbs are grown in containers it is usually only for a single season; close planting is recommended in this instance to ensure maximum impact. It is natural to want to space out your investment, with the bulbs covering a large area, but real impact comes from close planting with the bulbs almost touching.

Close grouping is particularly important with single-subject plants, but wider spacing is sufficient if they are interplanted with other bulbs, or spring-bedding plants such as pansies or forget-me-nots.

Big bulbs

With true bulbs, size is important because the dimensions usually determine the flower size. The size of some bulbs, such as hyacinths, may be stated in the catalogue or on the packet. Hyacinths with a 16–17cm (6½–7in) circumference are perfectly adequate for a general garden display,

even though the flower spikes will be relatively small and sparse. Those used for indoor pots are usually no more than 18cm (7in) bulbs, while top-size bulbs, with the biggest and best spikes, are 18cm (7in) or more. For a showy display in containers, buy the largest size you can afford. The size of a tuber, corm or rhizome is not an indication of its flower size.

■ LEFT
A container like this, packed with a brilliant tulip such as the muti-flowered single late 'Red Georgette', will make a commanding focal point.

■ BELOW
Plastic pots can be surprisingly acceptable if the flowers are stunning. This corner of a patio is vibrant with spring colour.

Bulbs for the home

Very few bulbs are true house plants that can be kept permanently in the home. There are exceptions, such as achimenes and hippeastrums (sometimes still referred to as amaryllis, which is strictly speaking an outdoor plant), but the majority of plants with bulbs, corms or tubers are very unsatisfactory if kept indoors permanently. The majority are also plain boring and unattractive once the flowers are over. They are best grown outdoors, or perhaps in a cold greenhouse or frame, and brought indoors for a short-term display.

Forcing the issue

Many kinds of spring-flowering bulbs are ideal for forcing – creating spring-like conditions indoors before they occur outside. This means you can have a continuous display of flowering bulbs, if they are planted in succession, from winter to spring.

For anyone with a very small garden, growing bulbs in pots brings the wonderful world of bulbs indoors at a time when outdoor gardens are looking decidedly gloomy. Some are so easy to grow that they are often given to children as an introduction to gardening: it is delightfully simple to grow a hyacinth in water.

Hyacinths, along with hippeastrums (amaryllis), are perhaps the most widely planted bulbs for indoors, but there are many others to be discovered and tried.

Specially treated bulbs

A word of warning is necessary if the flowers are required in early or mid-winter. Although some varieties naturally flower earlier than others, for out-of-season flowering the bulbs should have been specially treated. After lifting, they are kept in special temperature- and humidity- controlled chambers to advance the flowers buds developing inside the bulb. They are primed to emerge and flower much earlier than untreated bulbs.

The terms used may vary, but any described as 'prepared' or 'treated' are suitable for forcing. They must be planted soon after they come on sale, and usually by early autumn: if you plant late they may simply flower at their normal time.

■ LEFT
Hippeastrums (amaryllis) are among the most spectacular of all bulbs. The flowers are huge, and the growth rate amazing as the shoots emerge from the bulbs. In regions where frosts occur they have to be treated as house or conservatory plants.

■ RIGHT
It is possible to have tulips in flower in mid-winter if you buy specially prepared bulbs.

■ BELOW
Hyacinths *Muscari armeniacum* and *Scilla siberica* are easy to grow and very reliable. Hyacinths can even be grown in water.

Hyacinths

For continuity of flower, plant some prepared bulbs, and some unprepared.

If growing in special hyacinth glasses, ensure that the base of the bulb is just above the water and not in contact with it. Change the water if it begins to smell.

A special potting compost (soil mix) for bulbs is sometimes used to grow hyacinths in bowls without

any drainage holes, but it is just as easy to use ordinary pots filled with normal compost.

Daffodils

Some daffodils will flower if grown in water, wedged in position with pebbles or even marbles. A classic for such treatment is *Narcissus papyraceus*, popularly sold as 'Paper White', which has an almost overpowering fragrance, and the yellow 'Soleil d'Or' is a reliable variety – both have clusters of small flowers. Specialist bulb suppliers offer other varieties.

Fill the container to within 5cm (2in) of the rim, position the bulbs, then pack more pebbles or marbles

between them. Keep the water level (preferably rainwater) just below the base of the bulbs. Adding charcoal to the water will help keep it sweet.

Tulips

Plant as soon as possible after the treated bulbs become available. Timing is crucial, and may vary according to which country you live in, so follow any instructions accompanying the bulbs. They usually have to be potted early, being placed in a cool position in the garden to encourage root growth. When a shoot begins to emerge, keep in a dark place at about 18°C (64°F). When the shoots are about 5cm (2in) long, place in a light position.

Plant Directory

The following gallery includes some of the most popular spring bulbs for the garden, but space precludes mention of the many varieties that are obtainable.

Where appropriate, we have indicated the variety illustrated, but consult bulb catalogues for a comprehensive range of varieties currently available. A further selection of bulbs can be found at the end of this book.

Heights are only approximate, and may vary according to soil and site, and even variety.

■ LEFT
CROCUS CHRYSANTHUS

The first of the popular crocuses to flower. The species grows wild in Greece and Turkey, but the ones grown are the many varieties and hybrids (shown here is 'E. A. Bowles'). Colours include shades of yellow, cream, blue and purple, as well as white. Many have outer petals striped or flushed in a contrasting colour. Height 8cm (3in). Corm.

■ LEFT
CROCUS VERNUS

The true species is seldom grown; the hybrids, with their larger flowers, are the ones that are universally sold. They may be described as Dutch hybrids or Dutch crocuses. Colours include many shades of blue, yellow, purple, and white. Shown here is 'Purpureus Grandiflorus'. Height 13cm (5in). Corm.

■ OPPOSITE TOP
CHIONODOXA LUCILIAE

Sometimes called glory of the snow because it grows naturally in mountains where it flowers as the snow melts, this eastern Mediterranean bulb naturalizes and spreads readily. In gardens, it flowers in early and mid-spring, sometimes long after the last snow. Height 15cm (6in). Bulb.

■ OPPOSITE BOTTOM
ANEMONE BLANDA

This native of south-east Europe, Cyprus, western Turkey and the Caucasus usually has blue flowers, but some varieties are white or pink. Mixtures are popular, but a single-colour planting is usually more striking. The daisy-type flowers in early spring are best in partial shade or full sun. Height 5–10cm (2–4in). Tuber.

■ RIGHT
ERANTHIS HYEMALIS

The winter aconite usually marks the end of the worst of winter. There are variations, and some hybrids with bolder flowers, but the species gives a pleasing display if naturalized in short grass or among shrubs. 'Guinea Gold' is illustrated here. Height 8–10cm (3–4in). Tuber.

■ ABOVE
FRITILLARIA MELEAGRIS

In some countries this has the common
name of snake's-head fritillary; in others it
is known as the checkered lily. A native of
northern and central Europe, this charming
pink-flowering, dainty plant is best left
undisturbed in short grass, or in clumps in
a rock garden. There is also a white form.
Height 25–30cm (10–12in). Bulb.

■ ABOVE
FRITILLARIA IMPERIALIS

The crown imperial is a most majestic bulb – a clump in a bed or
border will stand out across the garden. A native of southern Turkey
and Kashmir, it flowers in mid-spring. Orange-red is the dominant
colour, though there are varieties with red or yellow flowers, and
some have variegated leaves. Height 1.2m (4ft). Bulb.

■ OPPOSITE
GALANTHUS NIVALIS

Snowdrops are known to almost everyone, even non-gardeners.
Despite their small stature their early blooming makes a big
impact. They bloom in late winter or early spring, depending
on the season. Shown here is the common snowdrop, native to
Europe, but there are many varieties and hybrids, some with larger
flowers, some doubles. For general naturalizing, however, the
common single snowdrop is usually more effective. Height
10–15cm (4–6in). Bulb.

■ RIGHT

HYACINTHUS ORIENTALIS
(SINGLE)

The species, which originates from eastern
Europe and western Asia, is not normally
seen: the highly bred hybrids, sometimes
known collectively as Dutch hybrids, are
the popular kind. Most are single, but they
come in a colour range that includes many
shades of blue, pink, purple, mauve, yellow
and white. Shown here is 'Jan Bos'. Height
15–23cm (6–9in). Bulb.

■ ABOVE

HYACINTHUS ORIENTALIS
(DOUBLE)

Double varieties have extra petals, but the
number varies. Some varieties have just a
few extra petals and may look like singles
from a distance, others have more fully
double ones with rosette-like, individual
blooms. Doubles are most effective when
grown in bowls or raised beds, where the
flower formation can be more easily
appreciated. Shown here is 'Hollyhock'.
Height 15–23cm (6–9in). Bulb.

HYACINTHUS ORIENTALIS
(MULTIFLORA)

Hyacinths sold as multifloras are ordinary varieties grown by the producer in a way that encourages the production of many stems (albeit with more widely spaced bells), instead of one stout, densely packed stem. Multiflora hyacinths make an impressive display, and some gardeners prefer their looser growth. Height 15–23cm (6–9in). Bulb.

HYACINTHOIDES
NON-SCRIPTA

The English bluebell, a common native of western Europe, is a well-known woodland plant. It will tolerate full sun, but does best in light shade. Blue is the dominant colour, but there are both pink and white forms. Plant 50–100 bulbs to 1sq m (1sq yd) to create a colony for naturalizing. Height 23cm (9in). Bulb.

HYACINTHOIDES HISPANICA

The Spanish bluebell is similar to the English bluebell, but has wider leaves and stiffer, more upright flower stems. Besides blue, there are pink and white forms. This is an ideal bulb for naturalizing in a shady or partially shady area near trees or shrubs. Height 38cm (15in). Bulb.

IPHEION UNIFLORUM

This plant from Uruguay and Argentina has delicately scented flowers, but unfortunately smells of onions if bruised. The flowers come in various shades of blue, and there is a white form. It is best left undisturbed to form a large clump. Height 15cm (6in). Bulb.

■ RIGHT

IRIS DANFORDIAE

This native of Turkey is usually the earliest to flower of the three dwarf irises described here, often starting in late winter. It is also the brightest, the vivid yellow signalling its presence across the garden. Because of its small size, the delightful scent is more likely to be appreciated when the plants are grown in pots to flower indoors. Height 10cm (4in). Bulb.

■ ABOVE

IRIS RETICULATA

The species is a native of parts of Russia, Turkey, Iraq and Iran, but the varieties and hybrids are most widely grown. They come in many shades of blue and purple, with pretty, yellow-marked beards. Shown here is 'Cantab'. Early spring is the main flowering time, though they can be made to flower earlier in pots. Height 15–20cm (6–8in). Bulb.

■ ABOVE

IRIS HISTRIOIDES

Native to northern Turkey, this tough plant may be mistaken for *I. reticulata* from a distance. It flowers earlier, however, often in late winter. The most commonly grown variety is 'Major' (shown here), though there are hybrids. Height 10–15cm (4–6in). Bulb.

■ LEFT

MUSCARI ARMENIACUM

The grape hyacinth, from south-east Europe and west Asia, is a most amenable bulb that seems ready to make its home anywhere. It thrives in most places and multiplies freely. It makes a pleasing edging plant for a bed or border, and is ideal for planting in bold drifts among shrubs. There are varieties in various shades of blue, including a double, all flowering in mid-spring. Height 23cm (9in). Bulb.

■ ABOVE
NARCISSUS (TRUMPET)

The trumpet narcissi are most instantly recognized as daffodils by the English-speaking world, and are synonymous with spring. Like all the other large-flowered daffodils, they are highly bred garden hybrids. They have one flower per stem, and the trumpet (technically called a corona) is as long as or longer than the perianth segments (the petals). Colours are mainly shades of yellow, cream and white; pink cups are also increasingly available. Shown here is 'Dutch Master' which flowers in early and mid-spring. Height 30–45cm (1–1½ft). Bulb.

■ ABOVE
MUSCARI BOTRYOIDES

This native of central Europe is blue, but the white variety 'Album' (shown here) is perhaps more widely grown than the species. It is best grown in a bold drift for impact, or interplanted among dwarf bedding plants such as double daisies (*Bellis perennis*). Height 15cm (6in). Bulb.

■ ABOVE

NARCISSUS (DOUBLE)

Double daffodils vary considerably in their petal formation and colour, but they have a special charm that makes them pleasing cut flowers as well as garden plants. The distinctive dwarf, all-yellow, 'Rip van Winkle' is thought to be a double form of *N. minor* var. *pumilus.* It grows only to about 15cm (6in) tall. Shown here is 'Tahiti' which usually flowers in early and mid-spring. Height 30–38cm (12–15in). Bulb.

■ ABOVE

NARCISSUS (LARGE-CUPPED)

There are many excellent varieties of these in the usual daffodil colour range. Large-cupped varieties are distinguished by having one flower per stem, and a cup or corona more than one-third the length of the perianth segments. Shown here is 'Professor Einstein' which flowers in early and mid-spring. Height 30–45cm (1–1½ft). Bulb.

■ RIGHT

NARCISSUS (SMALL-CUPPED)

Similar to the large-cupped type, apart from the size of the cup or corona, which is not more than one-third the length of the perianth segments. Shown here is 'Barrett Browning' which flowers in early and mid-spring. Height 30–45cm (1–1½ft). Bulb.

■ RIGHT
NARCISSUS (SPLIT-CORONA)

These spectacular daffodils are strange,
exotic-looking and often stunningly
beautiful. They are officially called split-
corona narcissi, but in catalogues you may
find them described as orchid-flowered,
collar daffodils or butterfly narcissi. The
corona (the normal cup or trumpet) is split
and reflexed. They come in all the usual
daffodil colours. Shown here is 'Cassata'.
Height 38–45cm (15–18in). Bulb.

■ LEFT
NARCISSUS (CLUSTER-FLOWERED DOUBLE)

'Cheerfulness' (shown here) is perhaps the best-known example,
popular as a cut flower and often forced for early indoor flowering.
The clusters of small but very fragrant flowers reflect the parentage of
N. tazetta. In areas where winters are mild these narcissi can be grown
outdoors like ordinary daffodils, but in cold areas tender kinds such as
'Soleil d'Or' require frost protection. 'Cheerfulness', however, can be
grown in many gardens. Height 30–38cm (12–15in). Bulb.

■ ABOVE

NARCISSUS POETICUS

Sometimes called the poet's narcissus or pheasant's eye, this elegant flower from southern Europe is one of the most distinctive of the tall-growing kinds. The very small, yellow cup, rimmed red or orange-red, looks like an eye set in the centre of the large, white petals. It is good for naturalizing or for creating a cottage-garden planting in borders. It has other bonuses, being fragrant and flowering late, usually in mid- to late spring. 'Actea' is a popular garden form. Shown here is *N. p. recurvus*, which flowers particularly late. Height 38cm (15in). Bulb.

■ ABOVE

NARCISSUS TRIANDRUS (HYBRIDS)

These hybrid varieties have clusters of flowers, usually with slightly reflexed petals. They are useful for the rock garden and containers, and make good clumps at the front of a border. They flower in early to late spring, depending on the variety. Shown here is 'Ice Wings'. Height 25–38cm (10–15in). Bulb.

■ RIGHT

NARCISSUS TRIANDRUS

This charming miniature from Spain and Portugal is one for the rock, or even a sink, garden. The small clusters of nodding, pale yellow flowers (creamy white in *N. t.* var. *albus)* with reflexed petals have a delicate charm. The species has been important in the breeding of some of our finest dwarf garden hybrids (see right). It flowers in early or mid-spring. Height 10–15cm (4–6in). Bulb.

■ ABOVE
NARCISSUS CYCLAMINEUS

One of the most widely planted species, this native of Spain and
Portugal has also played an important role in the breeding of some
of our most desirable dwarf hybrids (see right). Plant in drifts in
moist ground in partial shade, where it can be left undisturbed to
bring charm and delight to the garden in late winter and early
spring. Height 15–20cm (6–8in). Bulb.

■ ABOVE
NARCISSUS CYCLAMINEUS (HYBRIDS)

These indispensable hybrids, with their reflexed petals showing
the influence of *N. cylamineus*, are dwarf, compact, and early –
qualities that make them valuable in containers and borders.
'February Gold', shown here, and 'Peeping Tom' are among the
earliest to flower (sometimes in late winter), but others bloom
in early or mid-spring. Height 20–38cm (8–15in). Bulb.

■ LEFT
NARCISSUS 'TETE-A-TETE'

This is officially listed in a group known as miscellaneous, a
heading containing hybrids that do not fit into the other main
groups. Perhaps one of the best-known in this classification, it is
widely grown for selling in pots in garden centres, and excellent in
containers such as window boxes and troughs. It is also a first-rate
garden plant for a border. It can be made to bloom from late
winter to mid-spring. Height 15–20cm (6–8in). Bulb.

■ LEFT
ORNITHOGALUM
UMBELLATUM

Coming from Bethlehem and the Middle
East, and having star-shaped flowers,
this is understandably known as star of
Bethlehem. The flowers usually open in
late morning and close in the evening, but
it is a pleasing plant naturalized in grass or
among shrubs. It flowers in mid- and late
spring. Height 15–23cm (6–9in). Bulb.

■ RIGHT
SCILLA MISCHTSCHENKOANA

Sometimes still grown and listed as
S. tubergeniana, this delicate-looking scilla
from the mountains of northern Iran is
an ideal bulb for the rock garden, but also
grows well in the partial shade around
trees and shrubs. It can be brought into
flower early in pots. The normal flowering
time is late winter and early spring.
Height 10cm (4in). Bulb.

■ LEFT
SCILLA SIBERICA

A native of central and southern Russia,
this robust plant is utterly reliable and easy
to grow. It self-sows and is ideal for drifts
that can be left undisturbed. Blue is the
normal colour, with 'Spring Beauty' being
a particularly dark blue, but there is also a
white form. It flowers in early and mid-
spring. Height 10–15cm (4–6in). Bulb.

■ OPPOSITE
PUSCHKINIA LIBANOTICA

Native to the mountains of Turkey,
Lebanon and the Caucasus region, this
bulb flowers in early or mid-spring. Even
with minimal attention it will continue to
flower in subsequent years, and quickly
forms a colony. It may be found listed as
P. scilloides var. *libanotica*, which is now
its correct name. Height 10cm (4in). Bulb.

■ ABOVE

TULIPA (SINGLE EARLY)

Like all tulips listed in this chapter, with
the exception of *T. tarda*, these varieties
have been highly bred and do not appear
in the wild. Single tulips are the most
popular, both in the garden and as cut
flowers, and these early varieties are
especially prized. Shown here is 'Couleur
Cardinal'. They are ideal for beds and
borders, and flower in the garden in
mid-spring, or earlier if given protection.
Height 20–38cm (8–15in). Bulb.

■ RIGHT

TULIPA (DOUBLE EARLY)

Being compact, double tulips are ideal
for pots, tubs and window boxes, or for
bedding in exposed gardens. The amount
of doubleness differs among the varieties,
but all are generally long-lasting in bloom.
Shown here is 'Peach Blossom' which
flowers mainly in mid-spring. Height
25–30cm (10–12in). Bulb.

■ RIGHT
TULIPA (SINGLE LATE)

These tall-growing varieties are excellent
for cutting, and are also popular for
planting with late-flowering spring
bedding plants such as wallflowers, which
fill out and hide the bare, leggy base of
the stems. They flower in late spring.
Shown here is 'Queen of Night'.
Height 45–60cm (18–24in). Bulb.

■ ABOVE
TULIPA (TRIUMPH)

These mid-season tulips bridge the gap
between the early and late singles, and are
mainly the result of hybridizing those two
types. There is a huge colour range, and
many are beautifully marked or shaded.
They are ideal for bedding, and make
superb cut flowers. They bloom towards
the end of mid- and into late spring.
Height 38–50cm (15–20in). Bulb.

■ RIGHT
TULIPA (DARWIN HYBRIDS)

Derived from Darwin tulips and
T. fosteriana varieties, they are
characterized by exceptionally large flowers
on tall stems. For this reason they are ideal
for very bold spring bedding schemes in
gardens sheltered from strong winds. They
bloom towards the end of mid- and into
late spring. Shown here is 'Apeldoorn'.
Height 50–60cm (20–24in). Bulb.

■ FAR LEFT, CENTRE AND ABOVE
TULIPA (LILY-FLOWERED)

Distinctive and elegant, the reflexed petals are long and pointed, with the buds tapering towards the top. Tall, wiry stems add to the impression of grace and elegance. Shown here are 'West Point' (far left), 'Marilyn' (centre) and 'Ballade' (above). The open flowers are like large, colourful stars. These dramatic-looking flowers are suitable for late spring bedding in sheltered areas and also make superb cut flowers. Height 45–60cm (18–24in). Bulb.

■ LEFT
TULIPA (FRINGED)

The name of this group is descriptive: the petals are edged with a conspicuous fringe, and look equally stunning in the garden or as cut flowers. Shown here is 'Hamilton'. These unusual, attractive varieties bloom mainly in late spring. Height 45–60cm (18–24in). Bulb.

■ RIGHT

TULIPA (VIRIDIFLORA)

Sometimes called green tulips because they all have an element of green, they are popular with flower arrangers but also justify a place in the garden. The green is usually most pronounced in the yellow, white and cream varieties, but the green streaks also contrast well with oranges and pinks. Shown here is 'Spring Green'. They usually flower in late spring. Height 25–60cm (10–24in). Bulb.

■ ABOVE

TULIPA (DOUBLE LATE)

These tulips resemble the early doubles, but are often more fully double and taller. They are sometimes listed as peony-flowered tulips. Shown here is 'Angelique'. They flower in late spring. Height 40–45cm (16–18in). Bulb.

■ LEFT

TULIPA (PARROT)

Parrot tulips look like the clowns among tulips: showy and extrovert, big and attention-grabbing, with large, lacerated, wavy, crested petals. They are not to everyone's taste, but are seldom ignored. They make excellent cut flowers, but are well worth growing in the garden if a sheltered spot can be found as they are vulnerable to wind damage. They flower in late spring. Shown here is 'Apricot Parrot'. Height 45–60cm (18–24in). Bulb.

■ ABOVE AND RIGHT

TULIPA (KAUFMANNIANA HYBRIDS)

The *T. kaufmanniana* varieties and hybrids are sometimes called waterlily tulips. The long buds, often cream flushed with pink, open into stars of oval petals that expose different colour combinations. They can look like different varieties in bud and flower. Shown here are 'Heart's Delight' (above) and 'Corona' (above right). Their small stature makes them ideal for the rock garden and formal beds, and they are among the earliest tulips to flower, opening in early spring. Height 15–20cm (6–8in). Bulb.

■ RIGHT

TULIPA TARDA

There are many tulip species worth growing in gardens, and this is an ideal one to start with. Dwarf and compact, it will multiply into large clumps if left undisturbed. The flower stems are very short, and the yellow-and-white blooms appear to grow almost from the ground. Blooming in mid- or late spring, the plant, from central Asia, helps to extend the season for the low-growing tulips. Height 10–15cm (4–6in). Bulb.

■ LEFT
TULIPA (GREIGII HYBRIDS)

Varieties and hybrids of *T. greigii* are among the best of the low-growing tulips for early flowering. The colour range is brilliant and varied, the centre of the open blooms often present a striking contrast, and the foliage is beautifully mottled. They are suitable for containers and the rock garden as well as formal bedding. They flower in mid-spring. Shown here is 'Plaisir', one of the many varieties with striking flowers. Height 15–30cm (6–12in). Bulb.

■ LEFT AND ABOVE
TULIPA (FOSTERIANA HYBRIDS)

These hybrids have very large flowers, and the colours are usually strikingly bold. 'Madame Lefeber', also known as 'Red Emperor', is one of the best early red tulips, sure to give a dazzling display in beds or containers. Shown here are 'Madame Lefeber' (left) and 'Concerto' (above). Flowering time is early and mid-spring. Height 20–40cm (8–16in). Bulb.

The Grower's Guide

Buying bulbs

Growing bulbs successfully begins with the buying, and like most kinds of shopping this can be part of the pleasure. Deciding what to grow and where to plant is part of the anticipation that contributes so much to the enjoyment of gardening.

On the whole, bulbs are remarkably trouble-free – at least in their first year – but if they are to give as much pleasure for years to come, it pays to buy with care and give them the attention they deserve.

Bulbs are bought on trust – you cannot see whether the variety is

■ ABOVE
This kind of display is best achieved by purchasing pots of individual hyacinths coming into flower, then potting them up with some winter-flowering pansies. Otherwise it is difficult to be sure of different varieties of hyacinths flowering at the same time.

■ LEFT
If you need just a few bulbs, perhaps for containers or the rock garden, consider buying them coming into bloom in pots. The choice will be very limited, but the colour will be instant. This is a dwarf *Greigii* hybrid tulip.

correctly named, or know whether the bulb will flower well unless you are particularly experienced in buying bulbs, and some diseases may not be obvious until the plant grows (or perhaps does not). Once you have found a reputable supplier that you are happy with, stick with it unless you have to go elsewhere for a particular variety.

The easiest way to buy bulbs is from garden centres. You can choose and check the bulbs that you buy for condition, but the range stocked will be small in comparison with that of a mail-order specialist. There is also a higher risk of varieties becoming muddled, especially when customers can pick up loose bulbs and put them back in the wrong box. This is less of a problem with pre-packed bulbs.

Mail-order bulb companies are likely to offer the best selection, and usually have a larger choice of newer varieties. Do not assume the varieties will necessarily be true to name, however, as errors occur even from reputable sources. The distribution chain is complex and labour-intensive, so mistakes do occur.

Sometimes bulbs do get sent that are diseased and unplantable – make a point of returning them for a refund or replacement.

Mail-order bulbs should be unpacked as soon as possible, even if they cannot be planted immediately. Return any that are unplantable and ask for a replacement.

Some bulbs, like these snowdrops, can be bought in the green from specialist suppliers. These are lifted and despatched soon after flowering has finished.

A few bulbs are difficult to establish when bought as dry storage organs (for example, snowdrop bulbs and eranthis tubers), and enthusiasts may prefer to buy these in the green (with their leaves on, usually sold shortly after flowering has finished). They are generally offered by specialist mail order companies – look for advertisements in magazines in the spring.

Instant appeal

For a small premium, many of the more basic bulbs can be bought coming into flower in pots. They are available from most garden centres, and even some florists, in late winter and spring. They are generally, but not always, labelled with the variety.

Provided you buy bulbs when the blooms are just opening and not when they are towards the end of flowering, you sacrifice nothing in display terms and the results are instantaneous. Depending on where you buy, the additional cost could be minimal, and sometimes potted bulbs are no more expensive than buying the same bulbs dry in the autumn.

Planting spring bulbs

With the exception of the few bulbs sometimes transplanted in the green after flowering, spring-flowering bulbs are planted in autumn. Those prepared for early forcing indoors should be planted as soon as they are available, but those for the garden are usually planted once the ground is available. With formal beds, this usually means when the frost has killed the remains of the summer bedding, though when autumns are mild and frost-free it is desirable to clear the summer beds before the first frosts. This is especially true if the bulbs are to be planted between spring-bedding plants such as forget-me-nots or double daisies (*Bellis perennis*), as they are best established in their final positions while the soil is still warm enough for new growth.

Timing is less critical where bulbs are planted in groups on their own. Daffodils generally benefit from early planting, but they will still flower if planted in early winter, albeit perhaps a week or two later than normal. Tulips are usually intentionally planted late, generally in late autumn or even early winter. In very mild climates tulips require a chilling before planting.

Preparing the ground

Unless naturalizing in grass, prepare the soil before planting. If conditions are appropriate the bulbs will last for

Spring-bedding plants such as forget-me-nots help to fill in the base around the long-stalked tulips such as 'Warbler'.

many years; if insufficient care is taken they will put on an impressive performance for the first season, then disappoint, or possibly die out within a couple of seasons.

Selecting a fertilizer

Quick-acting fertilizers, especially those high in nitrogen which stimulate rapid growth, should never be used at planting time. The bulbs already contain the reserves they require to flower well in the coming spring. Feeding is best done after

■ LEFT
Mixtures of narcissi can often be bought cheaply, and they make an effective massed display if planted closely together.

PLANTING IN BORDERS

1 Bulbs look best in large clumps in borders, rather than in rows or rectangular blocks. After the ground has been prepared, excavate a planting hole large enough to take a clump of bulbs – it should be about three times the depth of the bulbs.

2 Space the bulbs evenly, but as an irregular group, not in rows. Space at the distance recommended on the packet for economy, and for a long-term display, as the bulbs will multiply. For more impact in the first year, space the bulbs closer but not touching.

3 Draw the soil back over the bulbs with a rake, being careful not to dislodge them in the process.

flowering to build up reserves for the following year's flowers.

Bonemeal is slow-acting and releases its nutrients over a long period. For that reason it is often used at planting time. Raking in bonemeal is not essential and may make little difference to the spring's display, but it will help to raise soil fertility over time so it is worth using. Wear gloves (latex or vinyl), when applying and rake it in before planting, at the recommended rate.

Controlled-release fertilizers, which only release nutrients when the soil is warm enough, can be used instead.

4 Rake the soil level, taking care not to disturb the bulbs if small kinds are planted shallowly. Then firm the soil with the back of the rake.

5 Use small canes to indicate where the bulbs have been planted if there is any risk of cultivating the area before they appear. A label will ensure you remember what the variety is when spring arrives.

Bulb combinations

Always make a point of noting plant combinations worth copying. These can be different kinds of bulbs together, or bulbs with other kinds of plants.

Attractive bulb combinations include hyacinths and *Scilla siberica*, *Narcissus* 'Jack Snipe' with *Scilla siberica*, and the Kaufmanniana tulip 'Heart's Delight' with *Chionodoxa luciliae*.

Plants with which to underplant bulbs include: polyanthus (primroses) beneath tulips, the red double daisy (*Bellis perennis*) with white, double late tulips, yellow polyanthus with blue hyacinths, blue pansies beneath pink tulips, and aubrieta beneath tulips.

For contrast, consider dark red tulips with pale yellow wallflowers; for a more harmonized effect, pale pink tulips with dark blue forget-me-nots, and for soft colours, pink tulips with yellow wallflowers.

Tall tulips are usually improved by being underplanted with forget-me-nots, which hide the leggy stems and often provide a backdrop of a contrasting or complementary colour.

Fully plant a small area at a time before continuing, otherwise it will be difficult to avoid disturbing the young plants.

PLANTING IN FORMAL BEDS

1 After clearing summer-bedding plants and forking over the ground, removing weeds at the same time, rake in bonemeal if the soil is impoverished. This is not necessary if the soil is fertile and the bulbs are to be discarded after flowering.

3 Spring-bedding plants can be bought from garden centres. Wallflowers are sometime sold in bundles without soil on their roots, but whenever possible choose plants grown in pots or containers.

2 If planting between spring-bedding plants such as wallflowers or forget-me-nots, plant them before the bulbs. Moisten the soil an hour or two before lifting from the nursery bed if you have grown your own supply.

4 Plant an area of bedding first, then position the bulbs between the plants. Work methodically, starting at the back, and planting the bulbs with minimum disturbance to the plant's roots.

In countries where winters are
sufficiently cold, such as the
UK and many parts of the USA,
tulips can be planted straight
into the ground, but in warm
regions such as California,
Australia and South Africa, for
example, tulip bulbs should be
chilled in the salad or vegetable
section of the refrigerator
for six to eight weeks before
planting. Ensure that they do
not freeze, and make sure there
is no risk of anyone mistaking
stored bulbs for edible crops!

■ ABOVE

Spring-flowering bedding plants such as
forget-me-nots, bellis and winter-flowering
pansies have been used extensively in this
garden to fill in between the bulbs. These
plants also help to extend the period of
colour, as they bloom for a long period.

■ RIGHT

Interplanting with other bulbs can
produce magnificent results, but it is
difficult to synchronize flowering times.
Try combinations that you know will work
– here, tulip 'Heart's Delight' has been
interplanted with *Chionodoxa luciliae*.

Planting a window box or trough

Fill empty window boxes with bulbs for a spring fling before the boxes are required again for next summer's bedding. Complex arrangements using several different kinds of bulbs can be disappointing unless flowering times coincide. A densely planted display of just one or two kinds of bulb is usually more reliable, being likely to give a bolder show.

■ BELOW
Hyacinths should be packed close together for maximum impact. Plant up each container with just one variety if you want to be sure of them flowering simultaneously.

1 Check that there are drainage holes, but cover them with a layer of broken pots or coarse bark chippings to ensure free drainage, and to prevent the soil being washed away.

2 Add enough potting compost (soil mix) to cover the bottom 2.5cm (1in). Provided the bulbs are planted out in the garden after flowering, old potting soil or garden soil can be used as the bulbs do not require high nutrient levels during winter.

3 To pack in plenty of bulbs for a bolder display, try planting in two layers if two kinds of bulbs are used. Place the larger bulbs on the bottom layer, then cover with more potting compost.

4 Position the smaller bulbs on top, between the larger ones below, if possible. It is easy to detect the noses of those in the lower layer. Choose, say, dwarf daffodils and scillas or crocuses, but avoid tall daffodils with dwarf bulbs.

5 Top up with more potting compost, firming it between the bulbs, leaving about 1–2.5cm (½–1in) at the top of the window box to facilitate watering.

Planting a pot or tub

Pots, tubs and urns can be planted in a similar way to window boxes. Use the bulbs in multiple layers if necessary, or interplant them with spring-bedding plants such as winter-flowering pansies, forget-me-nots or double daisies (*Bellis perennis*), or even dwarf wallflowers with late tulips. Your container will make more of a feature, however, if the bulbs are planted up with a few evergreens for winter-long interest. The proportions of pots and tubs make them more suitable for tall bulbs such as *Fritillaria imperialis*.

■ RIGHT
Large decorative pots make pleasing focal points, especially if planted with tall or majestic plants, such as the *Fritillaria imperialis* shown here, planted behind a large clump of narcissi. If necessary, there is sufficient depth in large pots like this one to insert a supporting stake in windy areas.

1 A small, inexpensive conifer will provide useful height to prevent the pot looking bleak until the bulbs come through, and you can plant it in the garden afterwards. Use a few small-leaved ivies to trail over the edge.

2 Space out the bulbs before planting, so that you can adjust them, if necessary, to ensure even planting.

3 Plant with a trowel, being careful not to damage any plant roots in the process. Make the planting holes about three times the depth of the bulbs.

The natural look

Bulbs naturalized in grass can look wonderfully inspiring, especially once they have multiplied and formed large clumps and drifts of colour. Daffodils are sometimes planted in grassland and in orchards, or on banks and roadside verges, to provide a breathtaking display in early or mid-spring. Planted *en masse* they create an eye-catching, yellow carpet.

Once planted, naturalized bulbs can simply be left to multiply, and only require lifting and dividing very infrequently.

Crocuses are normally to be enjoyed at closer quarters, but when naturalized they have an impact beyond their size. Some begin to flower in late winter and, by early spring, pools of yellow, blue or white announce in their own unmistakable way that spring has arrived.

There are many other bulbs that naturalize well in grass, so be imaginative and look in specialist bulb catalogues for further ideas.

■ ABOVE
Large clumps of daffodils look superb around a deciduous tree, and can add colour and interest to an otherwise bare patch of earth. Keeping the grass long here also looks more natural than several patches in the middle of the lawn.

BULBS TO NATURALIZE
Anemone blanda
Anemone nemorosa *
Chionodoxa
Crocus
Eranthis hyemalis
Galanthus nivalis *
Hyacinthoides *
Narcissus
* Best in woodland or beneath deciduous shrubs or trees.

PLANTING LARGE BULBS

1 Lifting the grass as described opposite for small bulbs is inappropriate for many of the larger ones, such as daffodils. These are best scattered fairly close together, to be planted where they fall.

2 Use a bulb planter, a trowel, or long-handled trowel if you find it easier, to remove a core of grass and soil. Make the hole about three times the depth of the bulb you wish to plant.

3 Sprinkle some loose soil around the bulb to ensure that there are no large air pockets around it, then replace the core of grass. It may be necessary to remove some soil from the base for the plug to fit.

PLANTING SMALL BULBS

1 To plant drifts of small bulbs, such as crocuses or snowdrops, lift an area of grass by making an H-shaped cut. If possible, use a half-moon edger rather than a spade, to ensure a straight edge.

2 Slice beneath each flap in turn, then roll or fold it back. If this is done carefully, the grass can be reinstated with minimal disturbance.

3 Loosen the ground before planting. For a small area, a hand fork should be adequate, but if the ground is very hard, use a garden fork. It is worth forking in bonemeal or, alternatively, a slow-release fertilizer at this stage.

4 To create a natural-looking group, do not plant in rows. Scatter the bulbs and only respace those that are touching, or to fill a gap. Otherwise, plant where they fall.

5 Large bulbs can be planted using this method of lifting the grass, but usually there is space for just a few. Use a trowel or bulb planter, making sure the bulb will be covered with about twice its own depth of soil when the grass is returned.

6 Firm the soil, compressing it, if necessary, to avoid a raised area when the grass is folded back into position. Relift to make any adjustments as required. Firm the grass down, and water well in dry weather.

Forcing the issue

One of the joys of planting spring bulbs is that you can enjoy them in mid-winter. This paradox is perfectly possible if you choose suitably prepared or treated bulbs sold for forcing indoors into early flower. Unprepared bulbs may flower a little later, but for true winter flowering plant only bulbs sold for this purpose. Plant prepared bulbs as soon as possible after they come on sale to ensure best results.

Hyacinths are perhaps the most popular choice, but try some of the others suggested opposite.

■ ABOVE

For a decorative effect, plant hyacinth bulbs in water in a glass cyclinder. The bulbs rest on large pebbles so that the roots reach down to the water below.

HYACINTHS FOR EARLY FLOWERING

1 If using an ordinary pot with a drainage hole, use a normal potting compost (soil mix), but for a container without drainage holes use a special bulb-planting mixture formulated for the purpose. In some countries this is called bulb fibre.

2 Place a thin layer of the potting mixture in the bottom of the container – many bulbs can be forced with surprisingly little root-room. Position the bulbs on top; an odd number looks better than an even one.

3 Pack more potting soil around the bulbs, but leave sufficient space at the top for watering. Do not worry if their noses protrude from the soil. Ensure the soil is moist but not wet or waterlogged.

4 Place the bulbs in a cool, dark place until the shoots appear. A suitable place is a cold frame where they can be covered with 2.5cm (1in) of sand or grit. Keep moist but not wet, and be very careful not to waterlog containers without drainage holes. A cool, dark cupboard is an alternative.

5 Check the bulbs periodically, and bring them into the light indoors when the shoots are about 2.5cm (1in) high.

6 Clean the container if it has been plunged outdoors, and place it in a cool, light position indoors or in a conservatory. Do not place in a warm room until the buds have emerged and are beginning to show colour.

OTHER BULBS TO TRY

Daffodils The cluster-flowered daffodils such as *Narcissus* 'Paper White' and 'Soleil d'Or' are extremely easy and reliable, but do not place them outside where they could be frosted. Prepared bulbs of ordinary garden daffodils are sometimes available, but they require careful temperature control.

Hippeastrums (amaryllis) These are not hardy and must be kept in warm conditions from planting. Follow the instructions on the packet.

***Convallaria majalis* (lily of the valley)** The treated rhizomes are likely to be available only from specialist bulb suppliers. They are not the easiest of plants to flower indoors, and the instructions supplied should be followed carefully. A refreshing, fragrant idea.

Tulips Prepared tulips can flower indoors from mid-winter to spring. Unless growth is carefully temperature-controlled, however, they may not flower when predicted.

■ LEFT
Lilies of the valley, *Convallaria majalis*, are deliciously fragrant, and can be forced into early flower indoors.

Propagating bulbs

Propagating bulbs such as hyacinths and tulips is not worth the effort for most amateurs, and special techniques for the rapid multiplication of narcissi are seldom necessary for small numbers. In most cases, it is worth paying for new, commercially produced bulbs to save the time, effort and space required.

There are a few simple ways to increase your stock, however, which can be horticulturally satisfying.

Division

This is the easiest and quickest method. If you divide large clumps of daffodils, crocuses or snowdrops, for example, they will probably flower with renewed vigour.

Bulbs from seed

Many bulbs can be raised from seed if you have a spare piece of ground where they can be grown until they reach flowering size. It is an extremely satisfying method of propagation that gives a sense of achievement that bought bulbs seldom match.

Highly bred varieties of plants such as daffodils, hyacinths and tulips will not come true from seed, and the results are likely to be disappointing. Leave them to the breeders or enthusiastic amateurs with the patience and time. Concentrate on species and small bulbs that grow reliably from seed.

Seed can sometimes be bought from companies specializing in the more uncommon varieties, but you may be able to harvest ripe seed from your own plants.

If saving your own seed, sow as soon as it is ripe; otherwise, sow bought seed from early spring to early summer. Sow in seed trays or pots, but note that they will require less maintenance if sown directly into prepared soil in a cold frame.

Alternatively, sow in pots and plunge them to the rim in the frame, or in a sheltered spot outdoors. Sow in sterilized potting soil to reduce the problem of weed seedlings.

Water, and keep the frame or pots covered with shaded glass or plastic until the seeds germinate. This may take weeks or months, but check regularly and keep the soil moist.

Space out the seedlings in a cold frame when they are large enough to handle safely, and keep moist until they begin to die down naturally.

At the end of their second growing season, plant out the bulbs in a nursery bed to grow on to reach flowering size.

■ LEFT
Bluebells are among the plants that can be raised easily from seed, and in the wild they self-seed freely. Seed is an economic way to raise large numbers of plants.

DIVIDING BULBS

1 Lift the clump when flowering has finished, but before the leaves have died back completely, using a fork to reduce the risk of damage. Try to avoid spearing the bulbs. Loosen the soil all round, then insert the tines of the fork beneath the bulbs to lift them.

2 Unless you require a large number of individual new bulbs, prize apart the clump into three or four pieces and replant immediately. They will produce good-size clumps that will look well established next season.

MAXIMUM MULTIPLICATION FROM DIVISION

To raise the maximum number of plants, grow on each bulb individually. Remove any small offset bulbs from around the base of the old ones, and grow them on for one to two years. Replant the largest bulbs in their flowering position ready for next spring.

Some bulbs, such as tulips, produce only a few offsets each year. Others, such as grape hyacinths (*Muscari armeniacum*), produce them in abundance.

3 Replant without delay, before the roots can dry out. Plants that produce small bulbs can be replanted with a trowel; a spade may be better for larger ones.

4 Firm the soil after planting, making sure that there are no large air pockets where the roots may dry out. Water in if the weather is dry.

5 Carefully fork in a general fertilizer around the plants to get the new plants off to a good start.

Bulb care

Like most plants, spring-flowering bulbs respond to a little extra care and attention. Although many will thrive and multiply without attention, most will flower more reliably if their basic needs are accommodated.

Never attempt to force the same bulb for two years in succession, although hippeastrums (amaryllis) are a special case and can be grown on to flower indoors for another year. Eventually, most bulbs are best discarded or planted in the garden after the first year's bloom.

HIPPEASTRUMS: GROWING TIPS

Hippeastrums (amaryllis) are tender plants often specially treated to make them flower in winter. To get them to flower another year, albeit a little later, try the following:

• When flowering is over, cut off the long flower stalk close to the base.
• Ensure that the potting soil does not dry out, and feed regularly with a liquid tomato fertilizer, following the manufacturer's instructions.
• Try to keep in a greenhouse or conservatory from spring onwards, or otherwise in a very light position.
• If you do not have a conservatory, stand in a light but sheltered position in the garden for the summer months, once all risk of frost has passed.
• Gradually dry off in late summer or autumn until the foliage dies down. Rest the plant, and do not worry if the soil becomes dry.
• Start into growth again by placing in a warm position and watering in late autumn or early winter.

SAVING FORCED BULBS

1 Indoor bulbs that you plan to plant in the garden should be looked after until they have been hardened off (acclimatized) sufficiently to be planted outdoors. Start by cutting off the old flowering stems, so that the plant's energy is not wasted on seed production.

2 To avoid the temperature shock of placing them outdoors, place the bulbs in a cold frame, or by the window in a garden shed or garage for a few weeks. Keep in a light position and ensure that the potting soil does not dry out. Feed once a week with a liquid fertilizer.

3 In spring, plant out in a border, or where they are to flower, retaining as much potting soil as possible around the roots. Apply a general, balanced garden fertilizer around the plants, allowing the leaves to die back naturally. They may not flower well the following spring, but should bloom again the next year.

Feeding and lifting

The best time to feed bulbs is when flowering has finished. From then until the leaves die down, the bulb builds up reserves of nutrients for the next season. Apply a balanced garden fertilizer around the plants and carefully hoe it in. Water in dry weather.

If possible, hardy bulbs are best left to grow undisturbed, but those used in beds that have to be replanted with summer flowers must be lifted.

Once the foliage has died back, they can be lifted and dried, ready to be stored in a cool, dry place until planting time in the autumn.

1 If the new ground is required for other plants, it may be necessary to move the spring-flowering bulbs before they have had an opportunity to die back naturally. Lift the plants carefully with a garden fork, damaging the roots as little as possible, and retaining plenty of soil on them.

2 Find a spare piece of ground where the bulbs can be grown on until they die back, and make a shallow trench with a spade. Gently slope one of the sides to rest the stems against.

3 Place the lifted bulbs in the shallow sloping trench, then return the soil to cover them. Water in well, and keep moist if the weather is dry.

4 Once the foliage has died back, lift the bulbs if the ground is required for other plants. Dry off the bulbs in a warm, dry place, such as a greenhouse, and allow the old stems to shrivel before cleaning the bulbs. Pull off any dead stems and the remains of old roots before storing.

5 Clean up the bulbs and place small offsets from the bulbs on one side to grow on in a spare piece of ground to reach flowering size. Store all the bulbs in paper bags (not sealed plastic bags), label, and keep in a cool, dry place, where mice and other creatures cannot reach them.

Pests and other problems

Bulbs are no more prone to pests and diseases than other kinds of plants, but at some stage trouble may strike. Usually only a few isolated plants are affected, but it is important to act promptly, as problems can spread if not controlled at an early stage.

Aphids

How to identify: The common greenfly can attack bulbs in growth, but blackfly can also be a problem occasionally. Although aphids normally attack the aerial parts, the tulip bulb aphid is mainly a pest of stored bulbs. *Cause:* Populations readily migrate to other plants. *Control:* Spray aphids with an appropriate insecticide. Dust those on stored bulbs with an insecticidal powder.

Prevention: As a preventative measure, spray any plants that have been previously affected by aphids.

Lily beetle

How to identify: The adult beetle is bright red, but the maggot-like larvae resemble grubs, covered with black excrement. Both chew and badly disfigure the leaves, and the larvae look unsightly. Although a major pest of lilies, it can also attack *Fritillaria imperialis* among the spring-flowering bulbs. *Cause:* Adult beetles over-wintering in plant debris. *Control:* Remove the beetles by hand as a first step; spray the plants with an insecticide to control the larvae. *Prevention:* Spray all lilies when the first beetle is seen.

Mice

How to identify: Remains of partly eaten bulb. *Cause:* Mice and other small rodents will eat stored bulbs and those in the ground, especially in winter or when food is scarce. *Control:* Use bait and traps. Place them where pets and wild animals won't be affected. *Prevention:* Keep stored bulbs in rodent-proof containers.

Narcissus fly

How to identify: The adult flies look rather like bees, but you are more likely to encounter their larvae – white maggots which feed on narcissi and hyacinths. The maggots will be found inside rotting or diseased bulbs.

Cause: Populations normally exist where narcissi and hyacinths are grown regularly. *Control:* Dig up and burn affected bulbs to limit spread. *Prevention:* Cover the ground with muslin (cheesecloth) as the foliage dies.

Slugs and snails

How to identify: Some underground slugs attack below the soil, but most damage is done to aerial parts. *Cause:* Endemic populations. *Control:* Use bait or traps. If they are a major problem, biological controls may help. *Prevention:* Good garden hygiene will help reduce hiding places. Encourage wildlife to control numbers.

Stem and bulb eelworms

How to identify: These are microscopic creatures, and it is the damage they cause that is noticed. The bulbs may be soft, and growth is weak, with leaves streaked or twisted. Bulbs most likely to be affected are hyacinths, irises, narcissi, snowdrops and tulips. *Cause:* Might be introduced in infected bulbs. *Control:* Dig up and burn affected plants. *Prevention:* Buy from a good source, and avoid replanting in contaminated soil.

Aphids are most likely to be a problem on plants grown in pots indoors or in a greenhouse.

The red lily beetle is attractive to look at, but can devastate your lilies and is difficult to control. It will attack fritillarias as well as lilies.

The larva of the lily beetle is extremely disfiguring and will eat leaves, leaving holes, and then turn its attention to the flowers.

Basal rot

How to identify: Affected bulbs are soft, and mould may be observed around the base. If the bulbs grow, the leaves are usually yellow and tend to wilt. Narcissi bulbs are most likely to be affected.
Cause: Might be introduced in infected bulbs.
Control: Burn affected plants.
Prevention: Buy from a reputable source. Avoid replanting bulbs in contaminated soil.

Botrytis (grey mould)

How to identify: A widespread fungus disease that causes a fluffy grey mould on the leaves, and especially on dying flowers. It can cause spots on the leaves, and can spread to the bulbs. Particular species of botrytis cause specific bulb diseases, such as tulip fire (see right).
Cause: Poor garden hygiene and failure to remove plant debris. Also overcrowding and poor air circulation under glass.
Control: Lift and burn if the actual bulb is affected, or the leaves are rotting. Otherwise, remove affected flowers, buds and leaves, then spray with a systemic fungicide.
Prevention: Deadheading once the flowers start to fade.

Bulb and corm rots

How to identify: There are many different rots that can affect bulbs, but it is difficult to identify specific organisms without expert knowledge. Never plant bulbs with soft or diseased areas. If not noticed, or if the organisms are already in the soil, patches of bare earth where the bulbs have not emerged are an indication, or plants may emerge with very stunted growth.
Cause: Might be introduced in infected bulbs.
Control: Do not plant suspect bulbs. Soak or dust bulbs in a fungicide before planting, and dig up and burn bulbs that have not emerged when they should.
Prevention: Discard bulbs and buy new stock. Do not replant bulbs in contaminated soil.

A vallota bulb with basal rot. Always check suspect bulbs by pressing the base, and do not plant any that are soft.

Tulip fire

How to identify: The leaves that emerge are distorted, and the shoots and flowers stunted. In moist conditions the leaves are covered with a grey mould with black fruiting bodies. Small, black bodies develop on the outer scales of the bulbs, which sometimes rot. This disease, caused by the fungus *Botrytis tulipae*, can be devastating in parts of northern Europe.
Cause: Most likely to be introduced by infected stock.
Control: Where the disease is troublesome, soak the bulbs in a systemic fungicide before planting (follow the manufacturer's instructions). Dig up and burn affected plants.
Prevention: Buy from a reputable source, and do not plant in affected soil.

This 'broken' tulip among unaffected plants is probably caused by a virus.

Viruses

How to identify: These are not visible, but the symptoms include streaked flowers, streaked or mottled foliage, stunted growth or distorted leaves.
Cause: Transmitted from infected plants by sap-sucking insects, such as aphids. Bought bulbs might already be infected.
Control: Dig up and burn affected plants.
Prevention: Control aphids and other sap-sucking insects. Buy bulbs only from a quality source.

Tulip fire is caused by a fungus. Destroy affected plants, and do not replant tulips in the same ground.

Calendar

Early spring

Bring in bulbs in pots and bowls for flowering indoors. Buy pots of bulbs coming into flower to fill any gaps or omissions. Deadhead early-flowering tulips and narcissi.

Mid-spring

Lift and divide snowdrops and winter aconites (*Eranthis hyemalis*), which are moved more successfully when in the green. Continue to deadhead. Start feeding bulbs that have finished flowering.

Late spring

Apply a fertilizer if this has not already been done. Continue to deadhead unless seeds are required. Collect seed from early-flowering bulbs. Sow as soon as possible.

Narcissus (trumpet)

Tulipa (single early)

Early summer

Lift and store bulbs when space is required for summer bedding. Sow seed. Divide and replant clumps that have become overcrowded. Continue to feed and water late spring bulbs that have not yet died down.

Mid- and late summer

Keep an eye open for pests such as the lily beetle and aphids.

Early autumn

Plant prepared bulbs for early flowering indoors. Send for bulb catalogues if this has not already been done, and place an order. Clear summer-bedding plants to make space for spring-flowering bulbs and bedding. Start planting, but leave tulips until later if possible.

Mid-autumn

Order or buy bulbs. Continue planting. Pot up non-prepared bulbs for indoor flowering to flower after the prepared bulbs. Check that bulbs being forced do not dry out.

Late autumn

Continue planting. This is a good time to plant tulips. Check forced bulbs to ensure that they are not dry.

Early winter

Finish planting. Check bulbs in pots and bowls for winter flowering. Do not allow them to dry out, and bring indoors when the shoots have emerged.

Mid-winter

Bring pots and bowls indoors to flower when ready. Ensure those still in pots in the garden do not dry out.

Late winter

Continue bringing early potted bulbs indoors. Place bulbs that have already flowered indoors into a cold frame, greenhouse or conservatory, prior to planting in the garden later.

Other recommended bulbs

Anemone coronaria

Anemone nemorosa

Bulbocodium vernum

Chionodoxa luciliae
'Gigantea Alba'

Allium karataviense This is a compact species with globular heads of light purple-pink, set against broad, greyish-purple leaves. Needs a sunny position and good drainage. Best at the front of a border. It flowers from late spring into early summer. Height 15cm (6in).

Allium neapolitanum A Mediterranean species with loose heads of star-shaped, white flowers in mid- and late spring. It is appropriate for a border or large rock garden, but not suitable for cold areas. Height 30cm (1ft).

Anemone coronaria The original species, native to Mediterranean regions, is not the one most commonly grown, but the florists' varieties which derive from it. De Caen varieties (like that shown above) have single flowers; St Brigid ones have semi-double flowers. Colours include shades of blue and red, with white. Height 15–25cm (6–10in).

Anemone nemorosa The wood anemone, from Europe, thrives beneath deciduous trees. The simple white flowers show up pleasingly against fern-green foliage. Height 10cm (4in).

Arum italicum A native of western Europe and parts of the Mediterranean. The strange arum-type, yellow spathes up to 30cm (1ft) long open in spring, which only appear reliably in a warm position in semi-shade, and are followed in late summer by spikes of red berries. This tuberous plant is grown mainly for its decorative

Camassia cusickii

foliage, however, which is retained through winter. 'Marmoratum', also known as 'Pictum', has particularly fine white and green marbled, arrow-shaped leaves. Best in moist soil, left undisturbed. Height 30cm (1ft).

Bulbocodium vernum Related to the colchicums, the crocus-like flowers that are associated with autumn, this native of the Pyrenees and Alps is a charming, unusual plant that almost always attracts attention. The funnel-shaped flowers are almost stemless. Height 2.5–5cm (1–2in).

Camassia leichtlinii

Camassia cusickii The large bulbs of this native of the USA can weigh more than 200g (7oz) each. The tall, blue spikes of lavender-blue flowers make an eye-catching clump. Ideal when naturalized in grass in semi-shade, it also makes a good border plant. It flowers in late spring and early summer. Height 75cm (2½ft).

Camassia esculenta See *C. quamash*.

Camassia leichtlinii Similar to *C. cusickii*, but with creamy-white to purple-blue flowers. Height 90cm (3ft).

Camassia quamash (C. esculenta) Similar to *C. cusickii* and *C. leichtlinii*, but shorter. It has bright violet-blue flowers, giving the impression of a blue haze from a distance. Height 60cm (2ft).

Chionodoxa luciliae 'Gigantea' Usually sold simply as *C. gigantea*. It has

Corydalis solida

Erythronium dens-canis

Erythronium 'Pagoda'

Freesia

larger flowers than *C. luciliae* (blue with a white centre); 'Alba' has white flowers. From Asia Minor, this pretty flower blooms in early and mid-spring. Height 15cm (6in).

Chionodoxa sardensis Another species from Asia Minor, this time with bright blue flowers and only a small, white eye. Height 15cm (6in).

Corydalis solida This charming, neglected plant is more at home at the front of a herbaceous or mixed border than as part of a bedding display. A native of northern Europe and Asia, the species is dull purple, but there are varieties with red or pink flowers too. It multiplies freely, and naturalizes well in sun or semi-shade. Height 15cm (6in).

Crocus tommasinianus This frail-looking, silvery-lilac crocus from the east coast of the Adriatic is amazingly tough. It is usually the first crocus to flower, often in late

winter. It is excellent for naturalizing in short grass. Height 10cm (4in).

Cyclamen coum Although the flowers resemble the tender florist's cyclamen in shape, these tiny flowers are totally hardy. They flower in late winter (sometimes before) and early spring. The flowers, in shades of pink and sometimes white, have a backdrop of marbled leaves. Height 8cm (3in).

Erythronium dens-canis The dog's-tooth violet, which is widely distributed in the wild from central Europe through Asia to Japan, is best naturalized in short grass. The flowers are usually pinkish-purple, sometimes white, and there are named varieties with pink and purple-pink flowers. They grow best in partial shade, and thrive in woodland soil. Height 13cm (5in).

***Erythronium* hybrids** Hybrids such as 'Pagoda' are generally larger and showier

plants than the species. They require similar conditions to *E. dens-canis*. Most will grow to about 25–30cm (10–12in) high.

Freesia Widely sold as cut flowers for their exquisite fragrance, freesias can be grown as summer-flowering garden plants, and as winter and spring pot plants. The outward-facing, trumpet flowers are usually single, but there are double varieties. They are not easy to flower as pot plants, so follow the advice on the packet carefully. A greenhouse or conservatory is required to get them to flower. Height 45–60cm (1½–2ft).

Fritillaria michailovskyi This distinctive and fascinating fritillaria, a native of Turkey, must be viewed at close range to be appreciated. The purple-brown, nodding, bell-shaped flowers are flushed bright yellow at the ends of the petals. Though sometimes

grown as a pot plant in an alpine greenhouse, it can be grown in a rock garden or even at the front of a border. It flowers in mid-spring. Height 15cm (6in).

Fritillaria persica The deep reddish-purple colouring of the flowers (plum-purple in the variety 'Adijaman'), on stiff spikes, ensures this species commands attention. A native of the Middle East, it flowers in mid- and late spring. It is best in a border, but requires a hot, sunny, sheltered position to succeed. Height 90cm (3ft).

Hermodactylus tuberosus (Iris tuberosa) Sometimes called the widow iris because of its sombre appearance, this plant usually appeals to those who like the curious. The flowers are translucent green with an almost black patch on each of the three large outer petals. They bloom in mid- and late spring, and have a delicate fragrance. Plant in a warm,

Fritillaria michailovskyi

Leucojum aestivum

Muscari aucheri

Muscari azureum

sunny position. Height 20–30cm (8–12in).
Iris tuberosa See *Hermodactylus tuberosus*.
Ixiolirion pallasii This Siberian plant is now more correctly called *I. tataricum*. It can withstand an average minimum temperature of -10°C (14°F). Since the leaves are grass-like, it is best grown as a border plant, in a large clump; the loose heads of blue, funnel-shaped flowers appear on long, thin stems and make attractive cut flowers. It flowers from late spring to early summer. Height 30cm (1ft).
Ixiolirion tataricum See *I. pallasii*.
Leucojum aestivum The summer snowflake, native to central and south-east Europe, is much larger and later than the earlier spring snowflake (*L. vernum*). The white bell-like flowers, in arching sprays, have green-tipped petals. Though this

species is often called the summer snowflake, it usually flowers in late spring. It is an ideal border plant, making a large, bold clump if left undisturbed. It can be naturalized in wild parts of the garden too, and looks particularly pleasing by a pond or at the edge of a stream. 'Gravetye Giant' is a superior form. Height 45–60cm (1½–2ft).
Leucojum vernum The spring snowflake is from central Europe. Smaller and daintier than *L. aestivum*, it has white bell-shaped flowers tipped green (sometimes yellow), and flowers in early spring. Height 15–20cm (6–8in).
Muscari aucheri (M. tubergenianum) This Persian grape hyacinth has sky-blue flowers at the top of the spike, and navy-blue ones below. It is an easy and reliable plant that makes a good display, whether planted for formal bedding or naturalized in a

wilder part of the garden. Mid-spring is the usual flowering time. Height 15–20cm (6–8in).
Muscari azureum The flowers of this muscari from the Turkish mountains are a light, bright blue that show up well despite the plant's small size. It makes a pleasing rock plant, but also looks good in drifts in a sunny or lightly shaded border. The flowering time spans early and mid-spring. Height 15cm (6in).
Muscari comosum 'Plumosum' A native to central and western Europe and Mediterranean regions, this unusual grape hyacinth has feathered violet plumes in late spring. It is sometimes called the feather hyacinth or tassel hyacinth because of its unusual heads of thread-like flowers, and is sometimes listed under its other varietal name of 'Monstrosum'. Height 20cm (8in).

Muscari latifolium This Turkish species always stands out and demands attention, despite its rather dark colouring. The bicoloured spike has pale blue upper flowers, and almost blackish-violet lower flowers. Those at the top of the spike are smaller than the lower flowers. Grow it in the rock garden or in formal bedding. It flowers in mid- and late spring. Height 23cm (9in).
Muscari tubergenianum See *M. aucheri*.
Ornithogalum nutans A native of Europe, this useful plant is perfect for naturalizing around trees and shrubs. It flowers well in partial shade. It is one of the easiest and most undemanding bulbs to grow. Its main flowering time is mid-spring. Height 30–40cm (12–16in).
Oxalis adenophylla A Chilean plant usually grown in the rock garden, but good in pots

Muscari latifolium

Ornithogalum nutans

Oxalis adenophylla

Trillium grandiflorum flore-pleno

too, it manages to combine beautiful, striking flowers with feathery-looking, grey-green foliage that is attractive in its own right. It is especially useful because it flowers in late spring and continues into early summer, helping to bridge the seasons. Height 8–10cm (3–4in).

Trillium cuneatum Trilliums are ideal for shady places in leafy soil, for instance beneath deciduous trees. They have their parts in threes: three-petalled flowers set against leaves arranged in threes. This species, from North America, is the garden plant usually known as *T. sessile*, but the true plant of that name is not as attractive and is seldom cultivated. *T. cuneatum* has dark crimson-maroon flowers, a colour closely reflected in the mottled foliage. Since the rhizomes resent disturbance, allow them to form large

clumps if possible. It flowers in mid- and late spring. Height 30–45cm (1–1½ft).

Trillium grandiflorum The wake robin is another North American species, and its requirements are similar to those of *T. cuneatum*. It has white flowers held well clear of the green leaves. This showy plant, blooming in mid- or late spring, is perhaps the easiest trillium to grow. *T. g. flore-pleno* has double flowers. Height 30–45cm (1–1½ft).

Trillium sessile See *T. cuneatum.*

Tulipa clusiana chrysantha The lady tulip, a species from

Tulipa kolpakowskiana

Afghanistan and the northern Mediterranean shores, has small, yellow flowers, flushed red. These tulips lack the boldness of modern hybrids, but have a delicacy that makes them appropriate for a rock garden. Grow in a sheltered, sunny position, in well-drained soil, preferably where they can be left undisturbed. It flowers in mid-spring. Height 20cm (8in).

Tulipa kolpakowskiana A species from central Asia and Afghanistan. It has small, elegant, slender, yellow flowers and pointed petals, flushed pink on the outside,

Tulipa turkestanica

in mid-spring. Height 15–20cm (6–8in).

Tulipa pulchella A species from south-west Asia, this very distinctive tulip is available in several varieties, though they are superficially similar from a distance. 'Odalisque' is pale purple with a yellow base, 'Persian Pearl' is magenta with a green tint, and cyclamen-purple inside, and 'Violet Queen' is rosy-violet. The less common 'Albocaerulea' is white with a blue base. It flowers in early to mid-spring. Height 10–15cm (4–6in).

Tulipa turkestanica A distinctive species from central Asia, with multi-packed heads of ivory flowers with a yellow base, flushed grey-green on the outside. This is not a bright tulip, but it creates plenty of impact if planted in a dense drift. It flowers in early to mid-spring. Height 15–23cm (6–9in).

Hyacinthus orientalis

Tulipa 'Queen of Night'

ACKNOWLEDGEMENTS

The publisher would like to thank the
following people for their help in the
production of this book: Chenies Manor,
Rickmansworth, Herts; The Royal Botanic
Gardens, Kew; Keukenhof Gardens, Lisse,
Holland and Bloms Bulbs, Melchbourne,
Beds. We would also like to thank Peter
McHoy for loaning the pictures used on
pages 8, 10b, 11, 21t, c & b, 22l, 23b, 25b,
26tl & tr, 29b, 30b, 31tl, 32tr, 38b, 40t,
41tl & tr, 48t, 51tl & tr, 55, 56, 57, 59 1st
& 3rdt, 60 2nd & 3rdt and 62 2nd & 3rdt.

Index

Hyacinthoides hispanica